A Tale of Ancient Whiteness

A Tale of Ancient Whiteness

Shtiwi Al Githi

Translated from Arabic by
Mira El Hayek

Edited by Helen Wing

NOMAD
PUBLISHING

A TALE OF ANCIENT WHITENESS

Shtiwi Al Githi

This book was translated as part of the Tarjim Initiative

مبادرة ترجم

Published by Nomad Publishing in 2023
Email: info@nomad-publishing.com
www.nomad-publishing.com

ISBN 9781914325717

The Publishers would like
to thank the Harf Literary Agency

To all the friends ato all those friends

who haven't fallen from memory,

despite all the distances and years,

the ones who remain,

and those who are gone,

whiteness extends from you and to you.

The poems in this collection were written between late 2018 and late 2020, in cities across Saudi Arabia, and on some of its long roads.

Contents

Foreword

When Nomad told me they were going to publish a range of contemporary Saudi Arabian poetry collections, I was very excited. It would be a huge privilege to look through the window of poetry at a world with which so few Western non-Arabic speaking readers are familiar. I had little doubt that I would find the poetry produced in the context of the geography, history and culture of Saudi Arabia to be fascinating, unique and, very possibly, opaque to me. And I was also concerned that in a region such as the Gulf, so often plagued by the received stereotypical assumptions of outsiders, the voices of its poets should not be belied or misunderstood, especially if translation into another tongue threatened to bring with it contentions of meaning and lexical or ideological impositions.

I believe this collection of poets provides a fascinating showcase for themes both relevant and necessary for a greater understanding of Saudi Arabian culture. I discovered in it poetry of immense diversity in both form and theme: poetry about identity, isolation and relationships with family and friends, surreal poetry about one's relationship with the object world and with a metamorphic natural world, poetry about Bedouin culture and about the traditions of Arabic poetry and Arabic history and Islam, poetry about poverty, poetry steeped in myth and storytelling.

In *Emptiness in a Long Line*, **Mohammed Al Khudhair** warns us to stay true to ourselves in the face of the onslaught of the modern, the constant battering by the news and the awareness that time is a succession of moments and feelings falling constantly out of our reach. In *Development*, he shows us how the photograph creates the myths of our existence, making us conscious of how we see. For him, photos create a 'unique connection with things we see for the first time /

and how they transform into icons as wide as we can see.' In his love poetry, in *Return my Head to its Normal Position*, he documents in minute detail the anticipation of love, its ecstasy and the way the world transforms for the lovers and love's eventual disintegration.

In *A Life as Big as a Packet of Cigarettes,* **Al Hussain Moafa** protests, with a rare and gorgeous lyricism, the injustices of poverty and of a powerless, restricted life. In stark hopelessness he begs to reclaim some beauty in his life, 'Give me back my banned books. / I will return your chants and anthems. / Who among you cast this night upon me? / Lift me from the depths of darkness, / withdraw your slithering tongues, / like the threads of cassette tapes. / Give me back the words I wrote, / release me from this cell as wide / as a packet of cigarettes.'

In **Shtiwi Al Githi's** *A Tale of Ancient Whiteness* Western audiences have a fascinating glimpse of the subtlety and depth of a nomadic imagination, of the desert mind, forged in deep experience of topography, philosophy and knowledge of the

Quran and of the ancient traditions of Arabic poetry.

In *The Clouds that Pass*, **Atheer Al Nashmi** also mines the history of Arabic culture viewing it through a contemporary lens with often absurd and comic intent. His aim is to throw a light on the delusions we live by and the contradictions we inhabit.

And in stark contrast, **Hatem Al Shahri** in *I Know Well the Face of Despair*, looks despair in the face in his elegy and lament for language. His is a poetry of isolation and despair. And it is language itself that restricts the poet, shutting him out of a sense of joy or access to the sublime. And finally, in **Mohammed Ibrahim Yacoub**'s *A Place of Forgetfulness*, we encounter spiritual poetry in the tradition of the mystic, of Sufism. Here the poet yearns for the sublime in both divine and human love, plotting his exile on Earth as a preternatural expulsion from Eden, from grace, in the fall of Adam, 'I recognize every absence by its name. / I am exiled in loss, like Adam.' In this deeply religious poetry, poetry itself becomes an act of worship where the poet seeks the hidden depths of the soul, convinced that this world is but a shadow of true life, 'I am other than myself, my words not all I convey, / my desires not all I fulfil on life's journey every day.' His poems are often declamatory acts of prayer in praise of love, both divine and human, as he exhorts us to, 'Like the howling wolf mocking every loss, / elevate your spirit, to the sky's pure gloss!' His poetry reverberates with the tradition of a thousand years of mystical Arabic poetry as he protests our restriction to our fleshly mortal selves and begs us to to, 'Shatter the cursed clay and find a brighter way!'

Again and again, through these poets, the reader is given an impression of the immensity of space in both the desert and the sky, the great expanses of the geography of Saudi Arabia that free the humble human soul into a sense of belonging and indubitable emotional attachment to the place that is Saudi Arabia. Indeed, I have come to understand, I feel, a little of the spiritual pull that Makkah exerts in the world of Islam in these gentle, lyrical portrayals of place.

FOREWORD

The emotional complexity and intellectual sophistication of contemporary Saudi Arabian poetry offers a huge variety of poetic forms, including couplets, prose poems, fragmentary free verse and lyrical storytelling. The forms of Arabic poetry, so challenging to attempt to render in English, also serve an abundance of tonal variety for poets who speak with a tender humour, for those who struggle to express feelings of alienation or failure, and for those who inhabit the meta-literary realms of their ancient poetic tradition.

Most striking for me in each and every one though, is the plangent honesty of the poetic voices in this collection, which leads me to the conviction that the task of poetry, the adding of something new and beautiful to the world, is indeed achieved in this impressive, new collection of Saudi Arabian poetry in English.

Helen Wing

August 2023

WHITENESS OF A TIRED LIFE

Introduction

My name is Winter, a falling cloud

bringing with it the music of life and dance.

As their names fall into my notebooks

I gather them up though I wonder if

they knew their own fate or the ages

of those who could not be saved?

In the beginning, nomads roamed here

but now, no nomads remain.

If time overflows our story will unfold
before your very eyes and I will be there
lurking in the shadows.

Temptation

Between me and poetry
a life of seduction and desire,
my poems incomplete without it.

No water flows
through the images of our song
except to reveal
the secret of our nature.

Prayer

The verse unveils
what words alone cannot convey:
time curtails the shape
of our existence.
The verse holds
the secrets that hearts hide away:
while joy blooms, a wheat field
of happiness.
The poem opens
a window drawn by lips
and as death follows love
this testament of the poem:
sacred prayer.

Journey

I journey on,
uncertain of my path,
unsure where I belong,
the world around me
pressing in with force.
I rush along
with dizzying speed.
Illusions grow
and time distorts my view.

As I journey on old memories
become my home: I am a stranger,
my yearning heart a shelter.

A wilderness in every land
without its people,
a foreignness in every voice
without a mouth.

The distance grows
and days slip by
with each farewell.
The years give back the stories
we repeat, each one a salve.
Not every moment is a blessing,
not every tear is bitter.

We tread the sands of truth,
walk towards meaning in beyond.
Life overflows with images,
the eloquence of speech.

Oh land, tell us what voice
is calling
from the distant
red horizon!

If the sand of the land
is not a poem,
we must come
from poems
made of sand.

Identity

I am the lord of all I encounter
and lord of the winds that blow
with no allegiance to boundary or creed.
I am the lord of all travelers,
guiding their paths
to the moon and the stars.

As a child, I was nourished
by a queenly milk, and soon babbled
insights in clarity's corners
and quivered in front of beauty,
becoming the poem on women's lips.

I belong first to the Bedouin language
as it weaves through the desert
in the image of spring grasses,
as it calls the world into being
with the pronouns of life.
I belong to the language of heat,
cardamom and poetry
and dates in the winter halls.

I am the lord of love and song,
and the thousand prayers
of the humble at dawn.
I am the night and the morning,
I am the praised and the defamed.
I am the mercy, the anger and the grace,
the perfume of loyalty
and the longing for a child.

IDENTITY

I build ancient shrines from dreams,
distant blessings and memory.
I build myself in the questions of life,
stealing names in strange tongues
and arranging them like a song in the sky.

I am bound to the mist and the dew,
a loaf for the journey and an echo
in the ruin of the stars where I thrive.
I am a plant with a root in every query,
I spread the sands of truth in every valley,
watered from my ancestral well.

I am the lord of the overwhelmed,
of the pain in the eyes of the poor,
and the fulsome victories of fate.
I am the seed of the forefathers,
singing their last sagas in ink.

Alive in me are my people's oldest legends,
and the beginnings of the age of sorrows,
from the tales of Amro al-Ala, the treasures
of the builders from the sands of Nufud,
from depletion to the new age of space.

I am one of the last to embark
on this journey of life, so I fight
to evade the false ways.
I am the sword for the hearts
that can't fight in the final battle
of love and pride.
I am a candle for the tears
of the lovers and the dejected,
the lord of all who stand waiting
at every door of love.

I am the clay that forms the letters: W…I…N…T…E..R

Bedouin

Absence surrounds me,
yet I don't disappear.
Space distances me,
while I am near

and my presence
writes my leaving,
life flees me
as a stranger.

In shades of gray,
I roam familiar sands,
and famished
desert paths.
My caravan shines

a path of evening fires,
my horizon: a galaxy
of flaming stars.

I travel the holy
heavens at night
while wary stars
watch over me.

And when the night stars
fall away, the steppe
stretches out
in front of me.

The night wolves
do not fear my night,
nor hide their wild
in the sands.

BEDOUIN

Wolves feast
on my sorrows,
carry off
the pain of life.

I stare ahead.
The image of truth,
a metaphor, hides
the vast unknown.

My spirit,
tormented by cities,
by agonies,
longs for camels.
I am the string
of the grieving rebab,
and only the sunset
can spare me.[1]

My coffee,
tears of passion,
where rejected hearts
grow old.

In the sky,
under the watchful eye
of morning, Wadha remains
elusive, glinting in the light.[2]

She says from behind
the veil of day,
'Which misfortune
will you address today?'

And I strive, for her,
to live long, and to flee
the relentless Najd.[3]

BEDOUIN

My camel welcomes me
as kin, and sees
the burning sand
in me.

My heart's North,
my compass,
battles the South
for my heart.

The scorching sun
envelops me,
waiting for the cracks
to split my heels.
I am the desert,
all my steps a journey,
given meaning
by the storm.

I am the barren desert,
each burning moment
calling me towards
the setting sun.

Yearning begets
more yearning,
pallor drawn from the well
of my eyes.

I linger
with broken horseshoes,
for death is merely
lament.

If the horizon allows,

I shall embody

the core

of all meaning.

But if not,

under my spear,

a thousand stories

I'll unravel.

For when has adversity

ever been content

to leave humanity

alone?

Hanging On

He set fire to his soul,
borrowed the resurrection,
mounted the pyre,
as it blazed.

He sought the ancient ways
of death, but this death
rose up to his sword,
in flaming honesty.

If only, when life unraveled,
he could demolish
the foundations
and rebuild life anew.
Between him and time,

a form and a meaning:
when each tried to draw near
he sundered the divine.

From the essence of water,
from the wreckage of courage,
he poured forth
his virgin tears.

In the essence of fire,
he was consumed
until lightning became
the arrows in his hands.

Then joy rushed in,
a wolf unleashed inside,
to rid him of all pain.
And the horizon

folded over him,
a prophet promising
to reveal his dreams.

Growing sure in him
since as a child,
the sand had been
the beauty in his eyes.

He battled
the cities of the wind,
until he pitched his tents
high above the heat.

He came singing
and when he strayed,
maternal tears bathed
the earth beneath his feet.

He knew no ending,
except beginning ....
and death, the sign.

Changing
all the rules of life,
resurrection extended
through his hands.

In words of the old and wise,
grandfather says 'For the nation
to persist and thrive, my child,
let history pave the way.'

He tells me the homelands
of desire have departed,
that with the sunset we know
nothing of tomorrow,

that the prayer beads of this life
have only loosened to announce
the workings of eternity.

'And this soil, this salt,
part blood,
part memory,
passes through the family.

And the story of this land,
is the sand of love,
So, write a tale of those
who vanished in the mist.

For, I'm tired, my child
from what life has done to me,
So don't ask about
the weariness of my body.

My loss was already written,
as I believed the wishes
I made impatiently,
would be granted to me,

that my forehead would
never shine with sweat,
except to draw grass along
the veins of my hands!

I'm tired and this man
whose blood runs in you,
still refuses to bow
to anyone but god.

I carried the night stars,
on my shoulder,
and went in search

of the enchantress of eternity.

When life brought
my caravan to its knees,
my camel began to rest
on the blade of envy.

I'm stepping out
of countless wars, my child
and yet I find no place
to rest my sorrows.

I granted the desert a rhyme,
until my tongue burned,
until TB got the best of me,
settling in my liver.

Oh, fever and pain!
There was always
potential in revolution
even when we slept on stakes.

Oh, life has slipped away,
returning bowed,
among the othering days
of melancholy!

So, gather your prayers,
for our time is fleeting,
and death spares no hesitation.

Become a solace for a tired heart,
where life once bloomed,
and as I offer it now to you, my child!'

What Ibn Zuraiq al-Baghdadi did not Say

Poetry, unaware,
what challenges it may face?
Opposites unite:
a dream and its demise.

Its meaning draws him closer to its ruins,
As soon as he builds the worlds,
weakness returns to bring him low.

Yesterday distances a wish from his eyes,
and today tears descend his cheeks.

From pain he never rose,
except to face more woes,
Life's disappointment painful in his world.

He never shuts the door on dreams that haunt,
but with the wind's strong gust, he opens wide, undaunted.

In life's exile,
homelands within his blood find rest,
illusions gather in his hands, abreast.

He revolves in the orbit of meaning,
His days philosophize,
deceiving him away from joy.

WHAT IBN ZURAIQ AL-BAGHDADI DID NOT SAY

He interprets all he meets,
except a virgin language,
where he seeks the dew of meaning,
and returns it to him.

His ruins stand in the mist of clay,
his throne planted within the debris of the soul.

He never grasps life's purpose, its thrall,
except for the fearful things that may befall him.

In his heart, the thousand agonies of Baghdad,
From a thousand years, Death's voice raises him up.

His history, in all its blazing:
paradise, since Adam, closed to him.

Life is a riddle, and death, a mystery.
He wonders which mystery deceives him most.

Since the days of Cain,
time propels him towards absence,
the bird of separation startling him.

He faces mortality time and again,
depositing his heart.
His earthly unrest becomes his bed.

He sleeps, and life is strife,
questions of existence, rife.
Still, nothing can shape or control him.

Once he dwelled in the garden of eternity,
and his essence yearns for his origin, the clay.

The language of trees in his mouth goes astray,
his scruples cloaking his nakedness.

The vents of his soul leave his maze unsealed,
his clay scattered across the world, unrevealed.

He weeps for an Andalusia nestled in his heart,
where an ancient dream was lost,
and he tried to capture it on the canvas of his days.

The pursuit of his paradise,
to build a homeland from the essence of life,
the free spirit's quest which leads to its end.

Semiotics

Speak as you may,
but do not heed words' sway.
In the shifting hues, find solace.

Life provides ample inspiration for a thousand poems,
with which poets ascend to reach the boundless horizon.

They crafted life's metaphors,
and interpreted the meaning of existence,
from which the water flowed.

This allegory, a story it did not create,
but named the secrets to illuminate.

Penetrating the virgin's truth,
when veiled by the pristine language of expression.

Words, exhausted of meaning,
and frequently, the fragments' reassembly falters.

In daily logic, a margin lies,
untouched by infallible poems' ties.

Even if the ancient perished in flames,
a phoenix arose from its ashes.

Not all who kindled the dark with light,
unveiled the mysteries hidden from sight.

For poetry is entering gardens
repenting of its desert arid deeds.

And you rearrange the stars once more,
so a blue star walks to you.

You rename the stars, to truly see,
how, without them, the sky lies feature free.

And you witness destinies,
running wild and untamed,
as your bright smile departs
and you speak to the days, as they drift on,
so many quiet moments wearing us thin.

Skilled in eloquence, a mere spark,
only to bring hope to your side,
as with your prophecies, an absence awaits,
beyond your wisdom, a lote tree... and a call.[5]

No longer confined in your extremes,
embrace your desires
for the storm that lies ahead!

Even if absence denies its serenity,
a wild tremor still shakes off your dust,
striking down all assertions,
and levelling cities and mysteries.

And reciting the Mu'allaqāt
with a bowed lute chanting wilderness paths,[6]

your chaos, the last of two clouds,
drops a green thought down beside you.

Hide not behind the tribe,
gather a tongue, that strangers applaud.

SEMIOTICS

This fire is the first discovery you made.
Don't extinguish the red flame, in your poetry displayed!

Love, as the oldest sin you committed,
and fall in love again for every gazelle is Eve.

Leave your garden, you only forgot,
so the poor could inherit passion's taste.

Oh Adam, left behind with your load,
the journey is too great, an overwhelming road.

Choose the anthem for those who return,
and tell them, your patience is but isolation and … and song.

End your prayer with wisdoms twain,
for aged caravans lie there, amidst the bloodstain.

For they all return from distant lands,
their names abound, with names it rains.

When the pit darkens,
You shine bright, you flare alight.

No annunciation in the garment's fold,
unless to ensure night ushers in daybreak,
so erase the past in your notebooks,
and rise like the moon, lighting the way!

Tale of Tired Dreams

To their details…

for those emerging now

from the pain of fever,

distribute your day

and make them stars!

Once, the earth's salt

served as a stepping stone.

shedding tears upon

their unambiguous speech.

The dreams write

the probabilities of absence,

read the agonies of evening,
your wound's a welcome balm.

Those walking through
the spaces of our dreams
tread on the tales
of heaven.

And those who say
at every occasion
'This life has passed'
are adding to your sins.

This life's a path
for those who've chased it,
even if the road
leads to a thirst unslaked,
and, too, for those who say

'If exile distances you,
we are a homeland
where you will never tire',

and those who offer
their heart a taste of sin
so we can offer them
more mercy.

From a thousand rhymes they flow,
performing the ablutions
of your ancient longing
with their songs.

These tired dreams
have a passion for all miracles
and since the moment of their meaning,
you have given them an ear and mouth.

So, we dream our wishes
on the pavement of our times
to belong with family
distributed in far off cities.

Dreams are so patient, that patience
becomes the marker of an age.
But who says that patience
does not suffer too?

In a thousand years
since the Mi'raj,
the prophecy says: time
is written for you to learn.[7]

And you walk in all directions
to see each way in the end
leading to
your funeral.

For life is broader
than a tale of tired dreams
So, record the details of those you have known
and extend to them a hand, the light of wisdom.

The Tiring Story of Ibn Al Rabab

He embarked on life's journey,
choosing the most difficult roads,
exploring every distant corner in his odyssey.
Every mirage was the horizon of his waiting
and behind him, the tears of maidens wearied him.

He went as a prophet goes, without guidance.
carrying the strangest among the prophets' sorrows.
He wandered long until he found no friend
other than his land, and he knew no lover
that could draw him close.

And he became like one who sold life,
emptying it of any meaning.
So as to settle and reclaim it?

He wandered this earth, without a destination
knowing that the end is the sound of a groan.
For there's nothing in this life but endurance,
and patience is essential, and if time
dries it up, it's still worth securing.
(Remember he who cried for his life
found nothing), but sand and poetry.

Good intentions are a trust we reap,
and fate decides according to
the discipline we keep: this the sin,
paths left behind not guilty.

His sin that as a traveler on this earth

he struggled, all his life, to stay the same,
unaffected by what time had got in store,
shoulders burdened by such longing.

And so, he set free the dreams of youth,
withdrawing to recall t
he birthplace of his memories
at the dawn of their creation.

And he started serenading
In the desert,
playing on a lute, saying
love was not his flaw.

You say though that longing
is the journey of the silent one
who cried when the stars
showed him his desires.

The daughters of the night
guided his steps
and fever slept in his heart
withholding his desire.

How I wish the tender branches
remained uncut by the caravan,
and how I wish the tender branches
drew the travelers near!

How I wish desire,
even buried in heart's core,
could fulfil its destiny,
its yearning on this earth!

And I wish desire
had dwelled long enough in his heart
to bring lost love back to him,

that he could try once more.

This heart traveled all over the land
but no homeland other than poetry
could fascinate him.

Destiny neared his gaze and death
bowed down before him,
offering him the choice...
He selected the finest,
for, as his life held no value,
he preferred to ask for it to end.

In the Margins of the Biography of a Madman

Oh mercy, I cannot fathom
why poetry has refrained.
Yet between me and the flute,
a melody of satisfaction resonates.

I proceeded alone,
and the steeds led me
on a journey of meaning,
through the vastness of space.

I am that madman,
propelled by intense passion,
walking a valley of desire and longing,

addicted to the dreams woven by metaphor,
recounting all that passes in the embrace of the poem.

And residing in this space,
I see nothing, but the story of days passing,
mourning what is gone.

Should my world crumble in your absence,
I will approach you like a lightning bolt,
ardent with yearning and radiant.

Oh, doe of fresh poetry,
feel the connection
with what was once acceptable!

Remove the remnants of worry
about my past,
for I am the ancient,

whose life is grieving!
I swear by your eyes
love was my fate.
I swear by your eyes
poetry healed and yet, sickened.

So, do not ask the madman
about his longing
for he was never far from your land

and he didn't know which land would embrace him!
Every God's country is a land
for those who have passed.

And not every Layla has Qays as her lover,
not every heart has been consumed by passion.[8]
Oh, my short life, be a poem born
as the bond between lovers is torn!

The Wager on Metaphor

To Mohammed Ibrahim Yaqoub

A poet and a poet

The days will not bloom
unless we bloom.

The clouds will not rain
unless we rain.

Words won't know the colour of the sky
until we colour it
with the colour of joy.

Things will not gain the splendour of their life
until we search for the secrets of their essence.
History will not write
any poem
unless it finds the pain of prohibition
in a notebook.

My master
and my poetry write us together –
(Do the poets ever depart) from a lineage?

We choose to make the wager of our metaphor,
where no single face of truth shall prevail.

We choose to doubt our names,
to recount the first biography
in epochs.

We choose to give the poems their feathers,
to become a bird
in a larger space.

Wondering about existence,
our fortune is that we see things
from a denier's perspective.

The questions within a poem may exhaust you,
But the end of the river of life wearies me.

In vain, we try to be a galaxy
betrayed by the rooted clay.

We are an open wound
The more the wound grows wider,
the deeper dives the dagger.

We will befriend the sorrows,
the faces of departure everywhere,
a passport to liberation.

We will arrange the old stories:
perhaps the beginning
was an emptiness of lines.

And we will demolish one meaning
to build another
and prepare chaos
for a thousand scatterings.

And we will cross the desert
without prophecy:
our destiny of the resurrection
is like a road.

We age,

as we tread our questions,

and our responses know

no answer grows weak or old.

We thought that time extended our lives

so we could become wise in appearance and ways,

but when we looked back,

the greatest surprise,

lay in our eyes,

that, the poets, have not aged.

THE DARKNESS OF SOLITUDE

A Gasp for a Night of Isolation

I converse with my solitude,
and answer myself,
opening windows to the constellations.

The horizon gazes at me,
with a thousand secrets,
and I close the womb of dispersion before it.
I surrender to the absence, the nakedness of the soul,
for there's no purity in the blood of the remains.

I shed two tears,
for my certainty,
But neither my Nile nor my Euphrates

is generous.

Resigned, I live long

upon a poem,

Shattering what remains

of my steadfastness.

I bring two stars closer,

to my tranquility,

ascend two ladders

towards my demise.

The night prolongs

the story's admonition,

So that silence can toy

with the mouths of the narrator.

We knock on a door of this age.

No one is coming back.

A GASP FOR A NIGHT OF ISOLATION

We have the traces of Jacob's silence,
and in the flutes, the sorrow of prayers.

We embrace,
in the sands of the wind,
an ancient voice
calling our wilderness pain.

The desert left us no meaning in life,
Except for the silence of truth.

It asks about the colour of our days,
But our colour has no miracles.

The mirrors converse with us:
How do we appear?
We answer: like a gasp in a song.

And the echoes of time
transforms me back to clay,
takes me back to nothingness,
a nebula enveloped.

If the dawn does not care
for death,
it's natural for my demise
to linger here.

No song for silent revelry
during the pandemic;
no festivity, celebration banned,
no new songs, no chants at all
on my destitute lips.

A GASP FOR A NIGHT OF ISOLATION

The door closes its panels,
and the heart cannot see its joy
in the streets of yesterday.

The heart beats from yonder,
but the gazelle it wishes for,
remains far away.

The air we knew
is strange,
and the eyes we loved
have faded.

The celebration had fallen silent,
and talk of gatherings,
as fear settles,
on beloved faces.

We keep our distance,
and now no fragrance wavers,
for a poem to stroll upon its scent.

The intimate void stares into us,
dances on its own,
our homes become a cave:
a tomb, it bequeaths our funeral song.

The kohl has bled away,
from the eyelashes of young girls,
and the newborn are no longer spoiled.

Oh, childhood fun,
a far-off mirage,
in a desert stretching
through the wilderness.

In the turmoil of our hearts,
a thousand questions,
and answers mere feeble wishes.

Cities strip themselves in astonishment,
and in anticipation of emptiness,
raises its shades.

Throughout time, we have recited
the silences of an era:
at night we read
tales of deceit.

We have persevered,
but we can't bear more.
We have to break free
of its chains.

Heaven on earth
is the story of people
who traverse vast deserts
towards us.

So although in the quiet corners
celebration sleeps,
Someday, we shall rekindle
their vibrant, happy zest.

Caves

Nothing behind the door...
our emptiness became a carcass
awaiting what is to come.

Silence is all you see in our eyes,
the silent last beat in the world.

These caves are rich in debris.
We step towards eternal dark.

Nothing conceals the truth of our nakedness,
except our yearning for it not to be so.
The White Bright of a Homeland

THE BRIGHT WHITE OF A HOMELAND

Country for Tales

If we must wake up

to the dream one day,

we will awaken to find a homeland

that renews within us

and runs in our veins with the saffron of story,

our future the roses of song.

If there must be a story,

it will be told

and we will tell it

above this earth,

and tell all those who have passed away

and all those who come after:

We stood here
and God grew us like lavender
and the earth shone within us
and we became morning,
descending from the balcony of the sky.

We tell all those who will come one day:
we have a homeland of light,
that in the sky of beginning we have a myth
written by the high forehead
in the depths of our pride.

We say:
our colour has the face of these winds,
and these sands,
and these mountains...
and we inherited the dew,
and the space,

and we rest on the slopes of the night.

We say:

we have a homeland in the valleys.

Yesterday is born,

and tomorrow,

and the present, all embodied in our blood,

like the color of the absence,

like the deer.

We have a homeland in verse,

where its hymns flourish,

And its caravans set out for a journey,

towards the sun,

as our voices rise in song.

We have a homeland that takes shape

among our lavender whispers,

in the rising flame of heat.

And it sleeps with the calmness of a maiden's eyes
that love the tears of a poem,
that guard the sleep of childhood,
and pour the kohl of romance,
upon a heart that grow between two syllables:
Lo and ve.

We have a homeland that takes root
its green, like a prayer,
and it dwells in the hearts,
that the dawn made,
the roots of its faith,
our hymns standing upright,
in the evening prayer.

We have a homeland that will write our story,

in the dust of the stars,

and will scatter its glory in space.

We have a homeland that leaks

its green into our blood,

to fix our flag like long spears,

above the mountains of loyalty.

Coffee from the Homeland

Here is the homeland,

with dreams and glory.

Here history writes our tale,

and sings,

sipping from the coffee of the past.

Its final meaning will come to light,

and here we shall be.

In every direction, we shall stand,

as horses, on glory's land, we run.

Our homeland seeps into our veins.
In our blood it is always young.

We set it free within our songs,
for its limit in poetry has no end.

A unifying force we possess,
awakening hearts from old to new,
reviving memories that coalesce.

From Mecca, a door wide and true,
open to heaven,
prepared and ready, we shall be.

The fuel of our hearts we bear,
a sea of dawn in which we share,
fondness for our deserts rare, and love.

For us, the cypresses grow tall,
transformed to clouds,
overflowing, exuberant with life.

We pour devotion into our homeland's soil,
and immeasurable and countless tears.

We've journeyed through our childhood days,
and our youth of sand, and now
the palm trees of time are gray.

And so we stand, as we have grown, dear land,
to bloom a pact in the heart's green girth.

For a splendid homeland will shine for us,
as dawn always comes for homelands.

The Home of Sand and Water

On the sand of meaning,

we inscribe it,

as stars ascend on horizon's ship.

Ancient, eternal on this earth

it finds its home,

bearing the weight of the unattainable,

with wings of its own.

In the desert of stories, it forms a cloud,

heavy with the rain,

that pours down on our intentions.

Within it, the poem descends, each ode,
residing in love,
refining it hereafter.

Journeying through the distant past,
reaching for a future yet to come,
which, endlessly, it seeks.

Residing in the middle of the heart,
like a spark, it lights a verdant glow,
whose path lies in the sky.

When every story stands in the mind,
the legends of eternity will seed it.

And in love, it has a lover's tale,
of walking on this earth: his, the sect of love.

From the source of light that circled Mecca,
the skies of truth illuminate his Yathrib.[9]

And in Najd,
the branches of lovers bloom,
And in its quest for love, every lover is honoured.

.

Rooted, it becomes
the fuel of our hearts,

and when it rains,
its water floods the desert,

seeping into the depths,
quenching the thirst of our wishes,
satisfying this hunger with love.

Oh, our homeland!
Dance of swords, I recite you
bringing joy to us and to you.

Life blossoms within.
Like sunrise it rises
and sunset cannot
touch it.

It runs over this sand
like a poem,
giving birth to itself
and to the essence of meaning as well.

Here ages sprout,
until the harvest,
Shoots of dreams grow
that it adores.

Here, the days have faith,
as if within the cities,
his playground will someday expand.

And the radiance of history comes to him in awe,
and it will write us in glory one day,
and we shall write it.

And one day,
a galaxy of stars will come to us,
all the prophecies of infinity we await.

And one day,
the sun will recite the verses of its glory,
leaping the span of its orbit.

And one day,
good people will walk this land,

to every new revelation that follows.

And one day,
the pure ones will come as angels,
overflowing with light,
their procession roaming the earth.

Oh, the one hidden,
within our blood,
illuminates our path,
for life has renewed its ambitions!

What Remains of Ukazi Poetry

To those who grew up with the Dhād, I came waving,
and behind my saddle, the she-camel of longing roams.[10]

I touch the essence of poetry,
as if to reveal all the meanings of the alphabet.

I travel through meaning,
(and the ruins of Khawla),
A prophecy from those who allowed the metaphor,
and waved.[11]

I entered their names one night,
And said to all the blossoming ones:
Bloom!

I set my ride in Ukaz,
and I am but a Bedouin,
beside whom the wind sails.[12]

Traveling far in memory,
bending to the present,
life overflows with poetry.

History passes me by,
a holy light,
granting me in the wind,
all that is not, usually, granted.

The days tell me
every story,
on this prophetic earth can be explained.

Tell me

the lovers' prayer is a metaphor,

through which all the doors of poetry open.

I am the first to come.

Behind me, caravans flow,

and this is the yearning passion revealed.

We came, the poets of Ukazi,

and in our mouths, the echo was born,

an ancient voice wrapped in expanse.

Here, a language with its eternity stretching inside us,

much like the final star glimpsed in the celestial skies.

Here, names recognize the hue of their tan,

and say,

'Oh, those who are heading towards the sun,

Make way!'

We stood,

the steeds of poetry racing around,

neighing, we came into being up on the peak.

We stood here,

our letters, our steeds,

as the voice of Ukaz, resounding through ages.

THE COMPLEXION OF A WOMAN

A Descendent of Water

A passionate brunette,
approaching and retreating,
space surrounds her,
and poetry,
and abundance.

The sea lends her features of dew.
When she sings,
the perfumes of eternity gather in her
as she spreads the scent of youthful days and yearning,
her body swaying, a beguiling love.
The song on the strings of her youth,
a dervish merging with purity.

As as a verse or rhyme moves her to love,
her voice rises with a flame of passion.

And she walks asleep in her beauty,
so that the town may compete beneath her.

She never extends a hand to reach for a star,
but a hand from the Pleiades reaches down for her.

A prophetess, adorned with the verses of her allure,
a light illuminates our love and bursts into flame.

She casts her magic wand,
and miracles unfold,
in infinite number.
Descendant of water,
she never spills her allure,

like a timid cloud,

that never rains.

Her fragrance spreads verses,

a poem saying, ‘She is written’,

tomorrow foretold tonight.

A Life

She is a woman
who made herself a life

And she said,
'The meaning of your hands, the tenderness that shapes me
the meaning of your eyes, a dream that pulls me
into the story of us.'

And she said:
'The colour of your skin, the sands of our poems,
the longing of our rebab,
and the Bedouins leaving.

Zeidna

You were playing
and love played with you.
May God have mercy on love
if ever it brings you back!

Our longing rose
to the threshold,
so we obeyed your tears
as much as we could.

Whenever the agony
of love
intensified,
poetry spoke your pain.

As each day drew my pain in close,
it brought yours in closer still.

Desire

I want you

Always as the astonishment in my eyes

To write about you - seducing – poetry

I want you

two heavens above my hell

To flare up in the cradle of longing - ember

I want you

Oh early conversation in the morning!

And when night envelops you

I want you

Inebriated, twice, on my wine

On your lips, I drink my dreams

I want you

My laughter

Touch upon my forehead

I want you

And your embrace

The scent of you

I want you

Two stars that form my path

To pick the full moon from your hands

I fly through your skies, a bird of passion

Flying back and forth to you each dawn

I grow in your soil, a palm of passion
Bearing the dates of poetry

I want you...
If only this life knew
The age it has taken to walk to you

I want you
Nostalgia is the desert of my life
And love exhausts my waiting

Confession

I confess
I poured love into her mouth,
and drank the pure water
of Al-Kawthar.[13]

Was it a dream?
Yes, but in our blood,
a volcano of dormant love erupts.

In our absence and desire,
our playground is this metaphor,
your warm voice on the phone.

Behind our dreams,

our youth,

and love,

our certain inheritance.

Road

And she said:

'We will cross this long road

to our tomorrow, restless with waiting.

We will cross over one street…

two streets...

and we will board the first compartment of the train.

And one day we will walk the river to the sea

and draw the map of our life together

on the seashore and adorn it with shells.'

And she said… and she said many words
and a big dream.

But I had already crossed the road alone
and had not noticed
that I was going in the opposite direction of the train.

Anger

Do not be angry!

My longing was not in vain.

It was waiting for love to come.

I gifted your eyes

the unending steppe

for desire to live and grow.

From before this life, I fell

towards you from a thousand loves.

I'm still falling.

Do not be angry!

For the gardens belong to you

and I am the one flourishing in your footsteps.

Passing

The moon passed
over my song,
passed over the sky in the night.

It bent over me
speaking in the wind
shaking awake my heart.

The scent of your rose hair,
the honey of love on the tongue
of poetry.

If only I knew

whether beauty ever asks

how new life springs from love.

Strangers

You poured the water of life into my heart
though the echo dried up in my throat.

Strangers we were,
wandering away on the vast, long roads.

And when we returned…
between our lips, the longing
for the kisses of tomorrow.

Without this burning desire,
no beginning for our promises.

Reproach…

She is angry

and boredom is listed in her schedule,

'When did you leave my conversation, man?

When did you forget that time is but a scaffold,

with its ropes held by lovers' hands,

so they can reach their destination?!

This poetry has taken you away from me,

You once were the poem for me,

Now, I don't know to whom it speaks.'

'The poems,

Oh, mistress of my song,

A river flows so that the water flows away.

If you stand on a verse where I stumble,

the view is wider than where I fall.

The End

And we have ended
so that everything within us has come to an end
and the night has driven us apart.

There is no longer any point in remaining
No conversation…
No memory of our love.

No way to bring back out desire
No truce to dissolve the hue of not possible.

Every deferred love will wane, eventually
every passion withers and decays.

SHORT STORIES OF WHITENESS

Simple Folk

What do the simple folk do with their dreams
when life demands what they dare not desire,
as they stretch towards the waters of grace,
unaware of the thousand years
during which they have not drunk?

Forgetfulness

We forget
and life takes us into its shadow.
As we disappear
memories sometimes resurface.

We forget
and longing is a tale,
to be repeated
over and over again.

Even the road is sad for us,
knows we are lost
and will never reach the end.

Two opposites converge in our souls:

this longing

and the slow emptying of a life.

Questions

He asked, 'What is love?'
I said, 'It is a heart that wishes
to overcome the tremors of longing.'

He asked, 'What is sadness?'
I said, 'It is a translucent silence,
a burning ache that lingers.'

He asked, 'What is longing?'
I said, 'It is the long time
we spend wishing to meet.'

He asked, 'What is poetry?'

I said, 'It is the ancient voice

of the lovers' sigh.'

Stones

The stones of the earth
carried on our shoulders.
In the distance, time shows
us the journey between this life
and a fading memory...

We shall wait
for a tale we haven't told...
the thousand sorrows
of a time
eclipsed by mankind.

But for today what we carry,

and the width and expanse of our gait,

hold us to this existence, firmly in place.

Mirror...

An illusion there,
a voice here,
our mirror
a limbo between us.

Two being mastering absence,
waiting for annihilation.

We walk on both banks of our river,
the river always unaware.

The afflictions of life separate us
but the song of hope brings us close.

A long time ago...

a long time ago, we knew life

and rejoiced,

our mother lost within us.

A basket...

For sorrow gathers pains

in a basket,

its pieces wet with tears.

It never tires in the toil of dreams

except when it weighs

the abundance of lack.

Spring

And Allah's grass sprouts

upon our ruins.

Not all land produces fragrant grass

But when life approaches its end,

it comes back to pour forth abundance

Longing

And in longing, I have a long life
and in the dew of my memories
there is an ancient place
where parting is too hard.

When I unravel a strand from the past,
my friends tumble from my grasp.

Nothing remains in the heart
to light the paths that brought us together
and nothing remains in the arms
of any embrace.

Denial

We didn't ask the earth about them...
If only they knew
that on every land, we plant dreams.

We didn't ask the night about them...
We erased every memory
And closed what had been seen.

Not every door opened in their direction:
My winds run high
to a life in the sky.

Return

Those who return after an absence
will come with fading memory
and a heart torn apart by loss.
They will come as a swing forgotten by a child
They will come as a song spoken by slient lips:
their longing, a mirage.

Escape

Those who flee from their time empty-handed
will come one day
filled by the paths of life,
will come victorious over time and memory,
victorious over crushing pain
and the defeats of love and song.

Loss

Wishes delayed...

What a life, this!

Delayed by the unfulfilled.

As I search for remnants

within remnants,

memory scatters them all.

Silence

Silence is the last thing we say.

Perhaps it leads

to meaning without words.

Oh, the old sorrows of Jacob,

his silence bequeathed to Joseph

the wisdom of the years!

About the Author

Shtiwi Al-Githi

Writer and poet, Born Ha'il, Saudi Arabia 1978

Published works:

The Peel of Civilization: Issues of Saudi Culture and its Transformations - Intellectual book 2011

No Shadow Follows Me - Poetry 2011

Fields of Change: Nations Lacking Questions - Intellectual book 2015

A Lifetime Wrinkled by the Poem - Poetry 2015

The Modernity of the Bedouin: The Anxiety of Identity in Poetic Discourse - Sulaiman Al-Falih as a Model - Critical book 2017

Twitter: @shtiwialgithi

Email: shtiwi4@gmail.com

Endnotes:

1. 'rebab' – a lute-like musical instrument from the Middle East and Africa.

2. 'Wadha' – girl's name meaning brightness or illumination.

3. 'Nadj' – highland province of Saudi Arabia

4. Ibn Zuraiq Al Baghdadi – the Abbasid poet

5. 'lote tree' – or Sidrat al-Muntaha, (Jujube) 'the lote tree beyond which none may pass', the boundary of the seventh heaven in the Quran.

6. The Mu'allaqāt is a group of seven long Arabic poems considered the primary source for early Arabic poetry. The name means The Suspended Odes or The Hanging Poems,

7. 'Mi'raj' – the ascent to heaven by Prophet Muhammad

8. 'Layla and Qays' – about the 7th-century Arabic poet Qays ibn al-Mulawwah and his Ethiopian lover Layla bint Mahdi. Layla and Qays, are childhood sweethearts but not allowed to marry. Qays (called Majnun, which means 'possessed') is seen as mad with love. When Layla is married off to another, he becomes a hermit, devoting himself to writing verses about his love for Layla.

9. 'Yathrib' – a city in W Saudi Arabia, the second most holy city after Mecca.

10. 'Dhād' – Arabic is called the language of the dhād, which is one sound that does not exist in other languages.

11. 'ruins of Khawla' – refers to the ruins that inspired the pre-Islamic poets.

12. 'Ukaz' – market place and site of pre-Islamic fairs and poetry contests in Mecca.

13. 'Al-Kawthar' – The Pond of Abundance that exists in Paradise in the Quran.